The

Wit and Wisdom

of

Donald J. Trump

by

R. U. Kidding

&

Noah I. M. Knot

This book is dedicated to all Americans who cherish the freedom of the press that stems from the First Amendment to the Constitution of the United States .

Copyright © 2018

Published in the United States by Esel Loch Publishing Co.

ISBN: 978-0-578-20131-3

1. Satire   2. Donald J. Trump

Printed in the United States of America

CONTENTS

INTRODUCTION

Hey folks, it's all here in this precious treatise. It took many months of hard work to tease out all the fantastic Trumpian material we present to you for your reading pleasure. Note that we have left a bit of space for you to add any new gems that The Donald drops on us.

Enjoy!

R. U. K.

N. I. M. K.

1

WITTY COMMENTS OF DJT

2

SUAVE
COMPLIMENTS
OF DJT

3

WISE
OBSERVATIONS
OF DJT

4

PHILOSOPHICAL INSIGHTS OF DJT

5

TASTEFUL
TOASTS
OF DJT

The
End

www.ingramcontent.com/pod-product-compliance
Lightning Source LLC
Chambersburg PA
CBHW071017040426
42443CB00007B/826